The power of you

Being a Carer for a Loved One

by Anne Jones

Published by Anne Jones

Email: anne@annejones.org
Website: www.annejones.org

ISBN 978-0-9573627-5-8

Anne Jones Books

About Anne Jones

Anne Jones has written six books published by Little Brown/Hatchetts on self-development and how to access your spiritual connections for happiness and inner strength. She lives in Burley, in the New Forest, UK with her husband Tony. She spends her time writing, giving healing sessions, creating podcasts and running a consciousness community – Conscious Cafe. She is the founder of the Hearts and Hands for Africa charity, helping people help themselves. For relaxation she walks the Forest with her Labradors, Lucy and Buddy.

www.annejones.org

Anne Jones Books

Introduction

I am writing this book straight from my heart and personal experience. I have always had a loving and close relationship with my mother, however, when she became disabled and sick this was tested and tried to the limit; as was my patience, my tolerance and my ability to give with love and without expectation. I learnt to walk the fine balance between giving and caring for another while thinking and caring for myself; to be there for a vulnerable and needy person and retaining my independence and freedom; to value the time with my mother but also find time for my own work.

My mother was given a maximum of six months to live so we brought her into our home to care for her last days. Three years later she was still with us! It was the most challenging but also the most rewarding time of my life. What I learnt has prepared me for my own old age which looms ahead and has already been invaluable for caring for my husband through a current illness. I hope it helps you through your own difficult and demanding days and shines some light to find joy and laughter amongst the anxieties and exhaustion you are certain to face.

CHAPTER ONE:

The Question of Responsibility

During her stay with us my mother contracted pneumonia and was taken into hospital. She was very poorly and neither the medical team or I believed she would survive – she had been diagnosed with lung cancer and she was already in her nineties at this time. But she managed to confound science and with her usual gusto came through. But she was more than a little annoyed at being in hospital and spent much of her time moaning, not about her health but about being away from home.

I had spent every spare moment by her side and I noticed that each time she said, "I want to go home," I felt a pain in my heart and my stomach churned. I sat there thinking, "why is this upsetting me so much; there is nothing I can do; she must stay here so why do I feel guilty? Why do I feel responsible for this?"

I realised that I did feel responsible; it was my fault that she was in hospital and didn't want to be there. How ridiculous! But that is absolutely what I felt. I looked over to her and took her hand and shared this with her. "Every time you say you want to leave it hurts me inside, I feel responsible for you being here and guilty that you are not happy."

She looked at me hard. "Well then, you are stupid!" she said. I laughed "Yes you are right, how stupid." She said after a moment's thought. "I'm not blaming you. I just want to go home". I said, "I know you aren't blaming me, so I don't understand why it makes me feel bad." As I pondered on this the tightness in my chest left and my stomach settled. I realised that my fear of her being unhappy had dissolved.

I considered the ridiculousness of this situation and shared my thoughts with her. "I have always felt responsible for your happiness." Which was true. Ever since I was a child I have felt it was my responsibility to make her happy but for no obvious reason; my mother was the least demanding and loving mother you could possibly wish for. She stared at me long and hard again, "Then you are VERY stupid," she said. I agreed. How very, very stupid to feel responsible for someone else's happiness. Quite the most impossible task! But a lot of us do in fact think we are in control of something that is not ours to control and which, in fact, we have no right to determine.

The question of responsibility will come up often

when you are looking after an elderly parent or relative, so I am starting this book by looking at this tricky question. What is your responsibility of care, when does caring step over into controlling and how can you manage without the burdens of responsibility bringing you to your knees?

Taking responsibility

I am always conscious to avoid getting involved with other people's affairs, decisions and life choices without their full permission. It is too easy to step over the line and become interfering and controlling but with an elderly parent, once they get fragile and unable to manage their lives for themselves, we need to step up and take some level of responsibility for their finances and welfare.

Financial affairs

Fortunately, my mother and I had a sensible conversation while she was still mentally able, and we agreed that she would grant me Power of Attorney so that if at any stage she lost her mental faculties through stroke or dementia then I could take over responsibility for her financial affairs. As it turned out this was a timely move and saved me a lot of fuss when she did get poorly; a time when visiting lawyers and signing documents would have just added to my stress. Even if you don't use the powers when you first get the document signed, I heartily recommend that you get this in place once your parents start to get fragile or even before.

Caring for elderly or disabled relatives is a very stressful role and you will want to do everything you can to make life simple, organised and managed otherwise your own health can be compromised.

Planning for the future

The elderly can deteriorate quite quickly and unexpectedly and, although you and your parent may have a coping plan in place, I think it's a smart idea to always have a strategy in place for the next stage. This may involve moving from home to a care home or bringing in care at whatever level is needed. If you have discussed the needs with family and other members of your care team then everyone including your parent will be able to move into the next stage without drama.

While your parents are still able to make their own decisions talk to them about their future care; who will look after them, will they go to a care home and how will it be financed? I hadn't done this and when my mother had a stroke we had the trauma of her illness plus these decisions to make. As I have domestic help my husband and I offered to have her live with us, which was her own first choice. I felt that I would be constantly worrying if she was in a home and I felt it would be far the better option for us both if I could supervise her care by bringing in help. Was that a good decision? I think it was the best for her as she had her family close around her, but it did put a huge burden on my shoulders and changed the dynamics of our home considerably. I don't have regrets as I loved my mother very much. However, unless you have tremendous support and the time and patience, I suggest you think long and hard about this option, it will seriously disrupt your life and be a massive challenge.

One Step at a Time

It's impossible to plan for every contingency. What suits the needs and requirements of your parent one day may change in a nano second! One fall and the complete scenario shifts. Once you have the broad idea of the way your parent wishes to go take each day as it comes rather than worry about the future. If you need an extra pair of hands hire them in, if you need a medical style bed hire it or get it from social services, if you have to deal with incontinency ask the experts – if I had thought about this particular subject on day one I may well have gone a different route but we managed and coped when the time came with the help of some proficient agency carers and I became an expert myself on protective pants and pads! Persuading my mother to wear them was another matter – she would sneak them off in the middle of the night and we would find them in the bedside cupboard! Some of the everyday mini dramas often became a source of hilarity.

Selling the idea of a care home

I think the words "going into a home" can be upsetting. They give the impression of being foisted off and put into an institution. Use a more sensitive way to describe the move – "we suggest you move to assisted living", or "let's take your precious belongings with you to a suite of your own", or "moving to a bedsit where you are supported without the worries for yourself or the family". Anything rather than the dreaded "we are moving you to a care home!"

Although we had neglected to discuss her old age needs fully I did know my mother's wishes for her funeral arrangements and this made it so much easier for me to make decisions knowing what she wanted, and I learnt the benefits of forward planning.

Worrying about doing the right thing and not upsetting your parent is one of the hardest burdens to carry even when there is a family involved. Having their approved plans in mind will save you many sleepless nights, and believe me, when you are the main carer there will be many of these anyway! Where possible chose their future with them not for them.

Choosing a Care Home

If you have reached the stage where a care home is the only option or the decision is made for your parent to move, now comes the next very tricky decision – which home? My mother in law went into a home and I remember the angst of the family choosing the right one. I am not sure there is the perfect place but if you focus on answering these questions:

- Does it meet their particular needs e.g. Disability, size of room, nursing care, mental health care etc.
- Does it suit you. eg. Financially, close enough for you and the family to visit easily
- Can it meet possible future requirements, e.g. nursing and full bed care, palliative care

- What are the reviews like? Bear in mind there will always be some dissenters
- Lastly and most importantly does it feel right? Intuitively do you feel good about it? Do you like and feel warm about the management team? Remember you will feel guilty no matter how good it is!

How far do you go in taking decisions?

Of course, there are no set rules and everyone's situation will be different, but I found that my mother, who had been a very strong-minded lady in her time and totally self-responsible, was quite happy for me to take over her life towards the end when she became very sick, but before those final months she got very irritable if I made any decision without involving her! So, my rule was to always ask her what she wanted and let her be part of every decision regarding her welfare. Her choice wasn't always practical, but I managed that by talking through the options and then, if she still wasn't on board with the best choice for all of us, I would make arbitrary decisions myself!

I have a friend whose mother's first choice is to stay in her own home with her daughter coming every day to do the housework, take care of her medications, arrange her finances and run her home for her! My friend tried to comply but was sick within months!

If your own wellbeing is compromised, you must step in and make decisions that are reasonable for you as well.

How responsibility can affect you

The energetic implications of taking on all the responsibility of another person looks like this: Your burdens will sit on your shoulders like boulders.

You will doubtlessly have sore shoulders and upper back pain! It is worth remembering that everyone has the right to live their life following their choices; that is how we evolve as souls and this rule includes old age and the way we die. Everyone has a plan for their life before they come to earth, so in those difficult days when the person you care for is struggling and you feel upset because you can only do so much to help, remember that this was part of their life plan. Give all the love and support you can but realise that you cannot make it perfect for your loved one no matter how much you would like to. Trying too hard and feeling responsible for every pain and hurt will destroy you and spiritually it's not your role. Give love, make sure they are safe and getting the best care available then step back. Sweep your shoulders and remove the burdens and keep your focus on your heart centre. Remind yourself that your responsibilities come from love not duty and the load will lighten.

So, to summarise:

- It's never too soon to discuss the tricky questions of finance, long term care and a suitable home
- Take care how you put your suggestions of a care home – if that is the best route forward
- Don't be scared to talk of the elephant in the room – discuss the future and engage them in the decision making while they are able

- Be realistic – if you have a family and or a job you cannot do it all yourself and you cannot be a full-time carer
- Remember to keep breathing and drop your shoulders!

We always want the best for our loved ones but it's important that we also take care of ourselves too, finding the balance is the tricky part and in the next chapter I will be discussing how important it is to get some help so that you don't shoulder the entire burden yourself.

CHAPTER TWO:

Getting help – the right kind at the right time

In the last chapter I addressed the issue of responsibility and how taking on the entire care load of an elderly or infirm parent can sit heavily on your shoulders. You will need to get help to save your own health and to get the best for the person you are supporting. The first step is to decide what help you need. Then be bold and ask for it, whether it's from the local council, a care agency or friends and family.

When my mother became ill and in my search for assistance I stepped into an entirely new world; the world of social services, Macmillan nurses, sleep in care, day care and the apparatus that is needed for someone chronically sick - from air mattresses to oxygen supplies. As soon as I offered to have my mother live with us my first port of call was the doctor's surgery. There I was helped with names of agencies and as my mother was diagnosed with cancer among other things, we were connected to the Macmillan Nursing support who were truly amazing. As my mother became more ill and frail so her needs grew, and I sought more care. Here are some of the things I learnt on this journey with her.

Compatible Carers

I quickly learnt that it was imperative to find carers and helpers who met the approval of my mother and who liked and responded to her too! Not only was this important for her happiness but the downside was that if she didn't get along with them I and the agency had to repeat the effort of finding someone new again and again. A girlfriend of mine went through five cleaners for her mother before they found one that met her mother's needs. Her mother found fault with each lady they employed until they eventually found someone who came from the same area of India as her mother; only then did she feel safe and comfortable with someone coming into her home. Forget about judging their attitude just find someone that suits them.

Everyone I know who has been through this process has agreed that finding the right carer is more important than finding just anyone to do the job and a little more time spent up front getting it right saves lots of frustration and heartache further down the line. Also, it is helpful to tell the carers a little of your parent's background and history for this can open doors to conversation and friendship. I was lucky, one of my mother's main carers became a close friend to her and our family; she was not only excellent at her work, but she also took an interest in my mother and read to her and listened to the life experiences. This took away some of the emotional burden from me and gave them both pleasure. When my uncle was in his frail years we found a volunteer from his local church who would come in and read the papers to him. They too struck up a close relationship and took away some of my concerns of his loneliness.

As in all situations, in life a little love goes a long way to easing these challenging times and the love can come not only from yourself. Set an intention to find the love for your mother or father and the universe will respond.

Act sooner rather than later

Several of my friends have tried to do all the caring themselves and where this may have started with weekly visits to do shopping, manage home maintenance, help with bill paying etc. this quickly escalated to the need for visits several times a week to cook meals and do cleaning and so on. Most of them have tried to do it all for far too long and made themselves quite sick; they sacrificed not only their own time but that of their partners.

We naturally give this care from our hearts, but we must always remember to honour our own lives and health.

Get ahead of the game and as you experience the first signs or stress and any sense of being overwhelmed by the work and time involved then make moves to get in extra help and be prepared to stand back a little and let others get involved.

Getting other people involved

The most successful situations of caring for a family member are where everyone in the family including teenagers and children get involved in the experience. There is a role for everyone and an opportunity for all to feel the reward of love and fulfilment that comes from caring for someone frail and dependent. A woman I know is a facilitator for organising family help for troubled teenagers. She gets everyone in the family together and puts on a simple buffet of food and explains the needs of the child and asks what each member of the family (and friends too) can do to help. This is a great method to use to create a sense of community and to find the help you need. Children can read to their grandparents and sit with them for a while each week, men can fix the things in the home and everyone can take turns in shopping. When a family is scattered weekends can be offered and there is usually someone in the family who can spare a little money to pay for professional help when it's needed. When a burden is shared it is lighter. Don't hesitate to ask for help and give others the opportunity a chance to gain something from the experience.

I am convinced that the growing number of elderly in our society is offering us an opportunity to spread love and compassion and to give us time to allow different generations to get closer. Apart from private agencies, social services and Macmillan nursing there are some new initiatives where an elderly person can share their home with a student who needs a bed in return for some help in the home. This great idea, which started in The Netherlands, has worked successfully in some care homes and is now available for private homes here too. It has the advantage of giving the elderly independent living for longer and affordable living for students and young people. You can google home sharing to find a not-for-profit organisation near you that organises the process for you.

Respite

If you do have to carry the main burden yourself make sure you give yourself a break from time to time and take advantage of the respite care that private and council run homes offer to carers. And don't feel guilty that you need a break – your health can depend upon it.

To summarise:

- Seek help before you are overwhelmed
- Look for professional help and social services
- Call in the resources of family and friends – let them also get the benefits of sharing and caring and don't be afraid to ask!
- Look for alternative ideas and sharing opportunities
- Don't be ashamed to acknowledge that you cannot do it all yourself.

Remember throughout this challenging time of your life to ask for help. It's spiritually empowering to seek help and be open to all opportunities that the universe offers; don't let your sense of pride, fear of rejection or a sense of duty stop you from opening your arms to allow love and support come into your life and that of your parent.

CHAPTER THREE:

Dealing with Guilt

Now we look at the inevitable consequence of having a dependant relative, whether you are the main carer or share the role with other family members or professional carers and nurses, there is bound to be a time when, however much you are doing, however much you give, you will feel pangs of guilt.

Feeling guilt doesn't mean you have done something wrong! It's the emotion we feel when we haven't reached our own expectations. It's very easy to feel that our efforts are inadequate. There are certain to be times when you feel you haven't given enough, done enough or shown enough attention. We normally set our own bar of expectation for everything we set out to achieve in life too high. It's a normal human experience. If you are a perfectionist or have any issues of self-worth or esteem then self-doubt and self-criticism will probably disturb your inner peace much of the time. You may also feel shame, which is linked to guilt, but reflects your own self-image in a destructive and toxic way.

When you have commitments to your family and work and to a dependant relative there will be times when you will feel torn in two directions. Some parents use guilt to manipulate their children; and as the elderly lose control over their lives they often resort to this to gain attention, support, assistance and in some cases, a sense of power. Be discerning when your mother suggests that if you loved her you would do whatever pleased her. Ask yourself, is she trying to make you feel guilty? If you feel you are being managed and controlled step back. Make your choices on what is best for yourself as well as your parent.

Anger

It is likely that you will feel anger from time to time and this too can build on your burden of guilt. When you are dealing with things outside of your control you will often feel frustration and anger; anger that you are in a situation that so limits your life; anger that comes from dealing with slow moving social services, lack of medical support etc. It's not always easy to contain this anger and you may find yourself getting irritable with the person you are caring for. My favourite way to vent my anger is to beat up a pillow. It can't fight back and its difficult to do it too much harm! It is also very satisfying to give it a good thump. See the appendix for a meditation to clear anger.

What guilt can do to you

There are symptoms you can experience that indicate that you are feeling guilt. Your guilt may come from a sense of not meeting your own exacting standards or you may be dealing with old suppressed feelings of guilt that have been with you most of your life; formed in your childhood, maybe triggered by a careless word from a parent saying you have disappointed them or let them down. Guilt and shame are held in your solar plexus which is the energy centre that also holds fear and anxiety (butterflies in the tummy); this same energy centre holds your WILL, inner strength and determination. So, fear, guilt and shame can affect your will and erode your inner strength, your ability to make choices and you may find yourself overcome by anxiety and worry.

Symptoms that indicate you carry guilt

- *Over-eating and addictions*

A strong pointer to guilt and shame is the constant need to eat and fill the ever-demanding sense of emptiness in your solar plexus; leading to weight gain, digestive and dietary problems, addictions etc. This hollow feeling can be fed by frustration and powerlessness caused by the futility that whatever you do is not enough to make your parent well and happy. To let go the guilt follow the releasing exercise at the end of this chapter then you may find you can manage your diet based on genuine hunger. Ask yourself before you eat – is this going to make me feel better for more than an hour? Understand where your feelings of guilt and shame may be coming from. If it's something in your past, then forgive and cut the cords to it. If it's coming from a sense of not doing enough for your parent despite all your best efforts, then cut the cords to your need to be perfect.

- *Pain in the gut*

You may feel pain and have physical problems with your stomach such as ulcers, indigestion, irritable bowel syndrome and other complaints in your stomach. This is caused by the tension that builds from the solar plexus energy centre when you are constantly experiencing fear and anxiety which are common side effects of guilt.

- *You sacrifice yourself to please.*

You feel the need to please and are looking for approval to negate your own disapproval of self. The long-term effects of carrying guilt can turn you into a doormat or a pleaser; someone who looks for confirmation and approval especially from parents. Realise that some people cannot show gratitude and as people get older sometimes their personality changes and they lose their own perspective and become demanding from their own position of powerlessness. Do what you can then step away.

What more can you do?

Meditation to release guilt – cut the cords and forgive

In this meditation you can cut the cords to your expectations of being the perfect carer/son/daughter and to the expectation of making your parent completely happy and well. You can cut the cords to aspects of yourself too; to shame, guilt, desire to be approved, your anger for being in this situation, food etc. Anything which you believe takes you from being present and content with yourself and life. Most importantly of all, you can dissolve any negativity caused by your thoughts about your parent that can turn cords of love into cords of stress. This stress stems from constant worries of your parent's condition and your inability to resolve the situation for them. You want the cords that connect you to your parent to be filled with love not worry, guilt or frustration. This exercise is great for clearing any negative energy that has developed between you.

- Before you start tie a thread around your wrist to represent the cord that flows between you and the person you are caring for. Tie another one to your expectations of perfection
- Write a letter to your parent expressing your love and asking for forgiveness for anything that you may have done to cause them distress or pain
- Write a letter to yourself, thank yourself for the gifts of love and kindness you have shared and forgive yourself for anything that you may have missed, forgotten or misunderstood in the care of your parent
- You can burn these letters or shred them, let the emotions attached go and allow yourself to move on

- Close your eyes and relax, take four deep breaths and drop your shoulders
- Cut the cords to your expectations of being perfect by breaking the thread
- See the cord that connects you to your parent and as you ask for forgiveness and acceptance from yourself cut through the cord (break the thread that represents that cord) and release all the worry and stress. Make a confirmation that love for yourself and for them will be your focus in the days to come. Accept that there will be times of frustration and upset but that the overriding emotion will always be love
- Finally ask for any help that you need. Ask angels, God or the Universe, whatever feels right for you, but ask for the support that you need through these challenging times

See You need to address your guilt and forgive yourself otherwise it can build and develop into shame which is very destructive, toxic and may feed feelings of low self-esteem and self-worth and ultimately lead to mental illness. The pain of guilt is described as karma in some belief systems and karma expects us to suffer for the suffering we have created for others. Karma can be released by atonement and retribution – it can also be relieved by forgiveness and love and, as we know, love heals. Forgiveness and love can come from the person you have wronged or from yourself.

If your sense of guilt comes from feeling you are not achieving your goal of making our parent well and happy then forgive yourself and detach yourself from impossible-to-meet expectations. The meditation exercise below can help you with this.

See the appendix for a meditation to clear karma and guilt.

To Summarise:

- Accept that you will feel guilty from time to time
- Step back if you are being manipulated by either your parent or by members of your family
- If you feel angry give yourself a break and release your feelings where you can't hurt anyone (including yourself!)
- If you have underlying guilt that goes back to childhood look for the cause and seek therapy

- If your emotions become an issue between you and the person you are caring for – set back and clear the cords that connect you

Always factor in your own wellbeing and happiness – a happy you will do more for the wellbeing of your parent than a stressed and miserable you! In the next chapter I will look at ways that you can keep yourself strong and uplifted.

CHAPTER FOUR:

Keeping Strong

Whether you have taken the responsibility of caring for someone in your own home, their own home or even visiting regularly in a care facility you will find the demands on your time emotionally and physically draining. You are almost bound to get stressed at times as you struggle to balance your life and cope with the underlying anxieties of your parent's condition and situation. You cannot govern the state of your loved one because there are too many factors that are out of your control. You can help and you can care for them but their state of mind, their health and medical situation and even their emotions are largely out of your control. So, it is imperative that you manage what is in your control and do your utmost to keep your own spirits high.

Here are some ways that you can lift your spirits and keep strong

Find your reason to re-focus

We always need a reason to change how we are and to let go old negative habits and attitudes. If you are spending most of your spare time thinking and worrying about a sick or elderly parent or family member you may have forgotten to care for yourself. You may think it selfish to think of yourself, you may have just got into the habit of putting everyone else first. One excellent reason to change this is to accept that you cannot help anyone if you are sick yourself!

Set your intention to care for YOU!

Firstly, set your intention to take control of your own emotional, mental and physical strength and wellbeing. Write down or say the words "I am taking control of my wellbeing and caring for myself from this moment on." This sets your intention and gives you focus.

Start each day with a Morning Ritual to protect and align your energies.

Start your day strength and positivity with this short ritual that will protect and align your energies. You can do this in the shower:

- Call in protection to seal your energy field and prevent yourself from being affected by those around you and the toxic energies of sickness and disease. I use the Blue Flame of Archangel Michael, but you can use white light, a bubble or golden pyramid. Say

"I am protected from negative energies" as you call in your protective shield

- Place your hands together in front of your chest as if in prayer and see your hands as the doors of your heart centre. Open them as you set your intention to open your heart to receive love and give love unconditionally. Repeat two more times
- Interlace your fingers and bring your hands up and above your head and as you do this say out loud your intention of connecting to your higher self. E.g. "I am connected to my higher self, my intuition and my personal guidance." Follow this little ritual of intention three times

For a link to a YouTube of this process – see the Appendix.

Schedule time for you

No matter how much pressure you are under to be available 24/7 its essential you manage some time for yourself. If there is no one in the family to step into your shoes consider respite care which you can find by googling your local services. You will need holidays to totally recharge your own batteries and you should set aside time in each day just for you to uplift yourself. Give yourself a set time each day if you possibly can, if you have small children when they have gone to bed might be an appropriate time. Depending on your circumstances and your own choice consider Yoga, Meditation, a TV program, a soak in a bath, a walk, run or cycle in nature, dancing to your favourite tracks, a visit to the gym or a half hour relax on the sofa with a book. If you schedule a slot each day you have a greater chance that the rest of the family and all those concerned will respect your ME time. If you give this up, you will be in danger of falling back into self-sacrifice which is not a positive state to be in at all! When my mother was in a critical state I would go to my greenhouse and plant seeds! This focus on nature and doing something positive got me through one of my worst times; with enjoyable results for the garden later!

Revitalising your Personal Strength and Will

Your solar plexus is the energy centre which holds your will and personal powers. The counterpart of this energy centre in the universe is the Sun which is a tremendous source of energy. When I get flat or low in energy I think of the sun and its amazing spirit and call that power to me by visualising a beam of golden light flowing from the sun right into my solar plexus.

For a meditation to make this connection see Appendix

Use Meditations to relax and uplift.

A meditation to relax your body.

- Stroke your own shoulders and upper neck and arms, say "I release all the burdens and tensions of my life, now right now right now." Put on some relaxing music
- Lie down and breathe in deeply four times; as you breathe out let go the toxins of stress and tension
- Visualise a white light in the form of a small tornado of swirling light coming into your heart centre and then see and sense this light flowing through your entire body clearing the tension in every limb, joint and sinew
- Deliberately relax your body from your toes up to your head. Clench your feet and toes then relax them. Clench your leg muscles then relax them. Clench your buttocks then

relax them. Scrunch up your shoulders then drop them. Clench your hands then relax them, tighten your arm muscles then relax them. Scrunch up your face then relax it

- Lie still and just let the music take you where you want to go. Take yourself to a favourite holiday destination or a favourite beach

A link to a YouTube of this meditation in the Appendix

To Summarise:

- Set your intention to be strong, balanced and care for yourself
- Set aside a time for yourself whatever the circumstances and stick to it
- Find a form of relaxation that suits you and your situation
- Meditate to keep yourself strong and relaxed

Caring for yourself is as important as using the oxygen in an aircraft before you care for your child. You need to keep up your strength and health to be an effective carer. So, don't feel that you are being selfish, don't feel guilty but ensure you and your life has balance.

CHAPTER FIVE:

Managing your Emotions

When my mother had a stroke, I felt my heart was splitting in two. The pain was unbearable, and I kept dissolving into tears. The pain was as strong as if she had died! But she hadn't, and I couldn't understand why my feelings were so intense. Because she was still alive although I could feel the grief, I couldn't share it so I tried to resolve it like a problem I that needed fixing! But of course, there is no fix for grief. After a while my focus directed totally on her care and my emotions shifted and became affected by her condition and her suffering. Her stroke didn't leave her impaired in her speech and she wasn't paralyzed, but she was never the same again. There were flashes of her personality and nature, but it was as though a vital aspect of her had already passed on.

Three years later she died. I wasn't in the room at the moment she passed but I was beside her seconds later. On her cheeks were the tears of release that showed me she had just gone. As I stood by her side I became aware of an amazing energy flowing through me; I sensed the wholeness of my mother's spirit filling me and I could feel her as she had been years before. Although I cried, I was comforted that she was leaving her suffering and I had a sense of completeness, as though something broken had been fixed, that a healing of some kind had taken place with her pacing. I asked my spiritual counsellor about this and he told me that my mother had been due to leave earlier but her heart connection was so strong to me that it had prevented her from passing over completely; seemingly a conflict between her soul's wish to leave and her heart's desire to stay. It would appear that much of spiritual energy had left at the time of her stroke as planned which explained my sense of loss and grief. The sensation I experienced when she finally left was the reunion of her spirit.

In the years that my mother spent in our care there were many times that my emotional tap switched on! Some good, some not so! She went through a time when she constantly called out "Help me, Help me." When I went to her side she opened her eyes and smiled; I asked, "what's wrong darling?" "Nothing" she said. "But you called out" I said. "Did I?" she replied! After ten times in a couple of hours I felt fit to bust! Yes, there are many situations that can cause you frustration, at times anger and of course sadness when a person drifts through old age and their mind hallucinates.

Dealing with your emotions

Suppressed emotions are toxic to your energy, emotional body and your physical state. I should have allowed myself to follow my instincts and grieve for my mother fully when I sensed her passing but I held back because of our cultural conventions. There will be times when you feel pain and emotional when others see no cause to be upset. Don't be affected by what other people say or think. If you feel emotions let them out and release them as soon as you can. If you feel like crying find a quiet space and have a good cry, let it out. You will feel sorry for yourself often, you are human and having to focus on another person's needs constantly is very draining no matter how much you love them. Allow yourself to wallow occasionally!

One day our carer came to the house and I flew out as she arrived and ran into the garden and screamed and screamed. I felt completely overwhelmed as though a million tentacles were enveloping and suffocating me. The screaming helped! If you don't have a place where you can do this, you can try thumping a pillow; that can help with frustration!

You will need to work harder at releasing any residual negative feelings If you are holding onto emotions from past problems with the relationship with your parent. Childhood traumas and difficult experiences cause us to compensate and adopt coping behaviour that can become habitual. These are much harder to change, and it can take longer to heal the deeper scars from trauma, neglect and lack of love. It would be beneficial to your emotional and mental wellbeing to clear these old hurts and scars while your parent is alive.

Give yourself time and space and focus on what has upset you in the past and reconnect to your deepest feelings some of which you may have suppressed for years but that affect the way you see and feel about your parent. Write down what you think and feel then burn the paper and allow the energies to transform into the light of the flames. This is a powerful healing process and something you can do over and over till all your angst and hurt has gone.

Despite all your love and patience there will be times when your emotions will get the better of you, and that is quite natural. Rather than beat yourself up, use one of these ways to help yourself through to calmer times:

- **Essential oils.** I love essential oils and I use them to change my mood. You can put some on a tissue and inhale when you need it; use on your pillow at night to help you sleep. Lavender is very calming, peppermint will revive you, rose brings you back to your heart and love, juniper and sage can clear your personal energy of negativity and citrus fragrances will uplift you
- **Yoga.** I have always found this a tremendous help to relieve stress and the build-up of tension. I particularly enjoy Kundalini Yoga as the postures and mantras hold specific intentions for healing and changing your mood, habits and body tensions
- **Exercise.** Its well established that exercise can help release tension in your body and calm your mind. Just focusing on your body for a period of time is a release from your daily commitments. Swimming, running, Pilates, aerobics and weight training are all good for expelling excessive frustrations and stress
- **Reiki and reflexology** are excellent therapies for clearing your energy and meridians

- **Sound therapy.** I found a couple of therapists locally that give Gong Baths that clear your energy field with the vibrant sound of huge copper gongs
- **Relaxing baths and massage.** Pamper yourself to release resentment and frustration
- **Meditation.** In the previous chapter I shared a meditation to help you relax your body. Here is one to help you to transform your emotions. You will need a clear quartz crystal for this exercise or, if your imagination is strong, then you can visualise one
    - Take a crystal or gem stone and hold it in your hands. You are going to use this as the focal point to deposit all negative emotions and feelings that you wish to heal
    - Sit quietly, breathe in deeply four times and hold your hands in front of you, holding the crystal in your hands
    - Say "I pass into this crystal all my anger, frustration, pain, sadness, all emotions I no longer wish to feel from my thoughts or from past trauma."

- Send love into the crystal to heal and transform those energies

  Use Reiki or any other healing you know or just feel your love filling it now

- Next, bring your hands up to your heart centre."Ibringthiscrystalandallitholdsinto my heart where it is transformed into love right now, right now, right now."

To Summarise:

- Be honest about your feelings – they are yours and you are unique so don't judge them or yourself for your reactions to anything that comes up
- Use this time to heal any old bad feelings there may be between you
- Heal old childhood scars and any residual pain you still feel from past traumas
- Take positive steps to destress and relax from daytodaybeforefrustrationsandresentments build up

CHAPTER SIX:

Healing emotions and fears

In this chapter we look at the negative and suppressed emotions of the person you are helping and how you can assist them in releasing and healing them. The elderly come from generations that were taught not to embarrass other people with their own feelings and are therefore often ashamed to share their innermost feelings so many are nervous to express their emotions or reluctant to engage with the emotions of others. Fortunately, we now live in more enlightened times and you can take advantage of the hours you spend by the side of your loved one and through discussion and sharing you can take the opportunity to help them heal any old hurts, rejections or traumas. By encouraging them to share old painful memories you can lead them to let go pain and resentment. Without judgement and with acceptance you can cast a loving perspective on their experiences and many emotional imprints can finally be healed.

Fear of Dying

My mother rarely lost her cool and when times were hard she was stoic, as many of her generation were; she rarely complained about her physical situation despite years of osteoarthritis. In her end years she had cancer, lung disease and heart problems as well as severe arthritis in her legs which she continued to endure patiently. However, the one thing that troubled her was her fear of losing her independence and ability to care for herself and when probed she admitted an underlying fear of death itself.

Unfortunately, her life went on far longer than she would have wished, and she did become dependent on care and she suffered a lot. I often wondered what was keeping her alive; why didn't she pass on to what we both believed would be a pain-free and beautiful existence? She had faith, she believed in the afterlife and the continuous journey of the soul and she had many loved ones waiting for her. I thought it might be her strong will and determination; her strong fighting spirit and reluctance to give in and give up the fight to continue her life. When I discussed this with her it was clear that apart from a fear of death which she couldn't rationally explain, she just didn't want to leave me. We both became quite emotionally about that!

To help take a more positive approach to the future I discussed the positives of passing on; apart from ending her suffering she would also be reunited with her loved ones; her mother who had passed on when she was just nineteen and whom she adored, her brothers and my father who she had loved passionately. I spent weeks sharing memories, going through photo albums and I put their pictures up in her room. We discussed the great welcome party she would have when she arrived. As a result, she had a lot of dreams about her family and after a while her fears lessened, she relaxed, and she seemed to lose most of her anxiety. When she finally passed away she was unconscious and she went very peacefully. At the celebration of her life party we had in our garden we played her favourite Glen Miller music and I saw her dancing happily with my father. It seemed there were parties on Earth and in Heaven that day!

Talking about death can help to uncover any exceptional fears for we all have a natural resistance and fear of dying. Rather try talking them out of their fears simply encourage them to share their anxieties then you can bring up the positives and share memories of the loved ones that they will meet again. It was wonderful for me to share so many of her memories of family members and discover the ones I had never met.

Guilt and Regret

By talking about the past, you can bring up any unresolved issues and suppressed feelings that need healing. My mother had a lifelong regret that as a teenager she hadn't been overly compassionate and caring of her father who had been immobilised with osteoarthritis, a condition she herself experienced later in life. We talked it through. After she had expressed her regrets and feelings of guilt I suggested she might like to follow a meditation to meet up with her father and I led her to a garden where she was reunited with his spirit. She had a conversation with him in her mind and asked him for forgiveness. His response was loving and compassionate - he told her there was nothing to forgive for he had never stopped loving her and he understood and accepted her love even when she was a teenager. After that her demeanour changed and she was far more peaceful. Do everything you can to help release guilt as it's the biggest emotional burden that a human can carry, and it can return life time after lifetime causing inner distress and pain.

Anger

Anger is another harmful emotion that should be cleared and released if possible. I asked my mother if there was anything from her past that still angered her and she became quite vitriolic about a past upset she had with one of her brothers. I encouraged her to vent everything she had bottled up over the years for the sake of the family peace. I suggested she let rip and she did! She enjoyed that! Afterwards we laughed at her language! She explained that although her brother had upset her it had never stopped her from loving him and it was a great relief to clear the anger at last. Another box ticked on the emotional clearing to do list! Anger is an emotion that needs to be expressed to release it, albeit safely and harmlessly. How wonderful to have an emotional detox – whatever age you are.

Empathy and kindness

It's easy to be affected by the anxieties and emotions of the person who you are caring for, but despite your compassion for their physical and emotional suffering try to be empathetic rather than sympathetic. A Samaritan's counsellor I know told me that when people call in they are taught not to sympathise – if a person is at the bottom of a pit they need a rope to help them out not someone who is above them in a good place saying how sorry they feel for them. I personally find it mildly irritating when people continuously ask me, "Are you alright?" or the dreaded "I am worrying about you". Although it may sound ungrateful, I would like to respond: "Please, don't worry because that will only make me feel worse because your anxious thoughts will not help and could lower my spirits even further!"

With empathy we see and feel when someone is unhappy or suffering so that we can step forward to give love and support. Your smallest actions can make an enormous difference. A hug, a squeeze of the hand can have a massive impact on someone who is suffering. When we are in our darkest moments these small gestures of connection and care have extraordinary significance. I still remember every moment in the past when a stranger has helped me, or a nurse has held my hand. Even if your patient doesn't respond because of dementia, depression or fatigue know that your kind gestures make a difference!

Keep yourself Clear

Dealing with other people's emotions and problems can be extremely draining so make sure you put yourself in a protective shield before you start these conversations. There are a variety of ways you can protect your energy field and I have an e-book Protect Yourself on www.smashwords.com that gives you plenty of options. The Egg is an easy procedure to follow and is particularly efficient for shielding you from other people's emotions. Simply use our imagination to see a large egg in front of you. It has a very thick shell that will shield you from negative energies but will allow positive vibes to come through. See a door in the egg and open it and step inside and know you are protected. Repeat this through the day especially when you are tired or the circumstances particularly draining.

To summarise:

- Talk about death and help alleviate any fears of dying
- Encourage sharing and expressing any suppressed emotions

- Talk about the past and previous generations
- Fill the room with photos of family and friends both present and past
- Use the smallest acts of kindness to bring comfort and relieve anxiety
- Always keep yourself protected from the negativity created by fears and anxieties

The hardest challenge during these times is to keep a balance between caring for your parent and caring for yourself but if you look for the good in the situation and relax and enjoy the lightest moments you will look back on these days with fond memories.

CHAPTER SEVEN:

Coping with Personality Change

A recurring topic of conversation with friends who have helped elderly parents has been about how to cope with their parent's occasional uncharacteristic outbursts and changes in personality. It's well documented that Alzheimer's and severe dementia can affect character and personality, but it seems that even low levels of natural old age or slight dementia can lead to some disturbing and often hilarious situations. I will share some of our experiences and how we have managed the often very upsetting changes to our loved ones.

Loss of perception

Even the most loving and easy-going people can change when they are sick or frail. My friend's mother had always valued her daughter's personal life, had never been demanding and I remember her as the sweetest of mothers. But in the last few years she has lost sight of my friend's needs and even though her daughter struggles with her own family life she is now expecting her to visit every day with an hour each way through heavy London traffic. She has turned down all requests to move closer to her daughter or to move into a care home. She seems out of touch with the reality of her daughter's life and the impact her demands make on her and her health. This is not unusual, and it does seem that as we get old, we can slip back into the dependency of childhood. How do you manage these situations without causing hurt and upset? It is a real challenge but with tact and diplomacy you must create boundaries that protect your own health and emotional state. You need to draw a line and express kindly but firmly our own needs and draw on alternative support and speak honestly and clearly how it must be.

Antagonistic and demanding

One of my friends has a mother who is becoming not only needy and clinging but also antagonistically demanding. She comes from a culture where it is expected that daughters should give up anything and everything to be a companion and carer for elderly parents. In today's age of single families and female independence it doesn't necessarily work for a daughter to give up her life for her parent's. When my friend tries to make plans for holidays and visits away her mother throws a tantrum using manipulation and guilt to get her attention. My friend has managed her situation well by protecting her energy before she visits so that her mother's hurtful words don't get through to her (she gets into a huge egg with a thick shell) and she insists on taking time away to recharge her energies and to give herself some peace. If she had succumbed to her all her mother's demands, she too would be sick by now and would have handed her own will and spirit entirely to her mother. I have helped more than one woman who has done just that; it's devastating to see a daughter who has passed over their life to an autocratic mother in the name of duty and love. It's essential to step back and understand that the attacks are not personal, they are the sign of a woman who has lost her power. It can be helpful to discuss the cause of their anger and lack of concern for you. Find out what would make them feel better; ask why they are antagonistic and without arguing with them listen and see if you can get to the route of their problem. But always remember to protect yourself, let their words go over your head (DUCK) and step back rather than get involved with an argument for this will drain your own energy and upset you.

Start off as you mean to carry on.

Explain gently and clearly just what you can and cannot do and stick to a plan. If you say you cannot come on Thursday evenings because of your art or yoga class don't sacrifice it unless you really, really must, otherwise you may be expected to give it up every week and you will eventually be taken for granted which will lead to resentment. Remember your parent may feel vulnerable and disempowered by their frailty and or sickness and they will do everything they can to gain energy and personal power, in some cases at your expense. If you have a selfish or demanding mother or father only you can manage the status quo. It's up to you to draw the line in the sand and dictate kindly but firmly how much you can or are prepared to give of yourself – only you can determine where your boundaries are, don't expect them to do so.

Outrageous outbursts

Certain conditions or illnesses can cause temporary changes of character. Sometimes this can be so outrageous that it's laughable, (try to find things to laugh about – it's a wonderful way to lift your energy!) At one time I had a temporary carer in to help me with my mother's care. Unfortunately, my mother took an instant dislike to the woman, who had been a nurse and, I must admit was rather bossy. Once she would have gone along with anyone who was helping but this time she let her feelings be known. "I don't like that one," she said to me in a very loud voice in hearing distance of the offending woman. I frowned and signalled to her to shush but she just repeated once again. "No, I don't like her at all." I apologised on her behalf and at first the lady carried on gallantly but after four days she threw in the towel. She accused my mother of being racist and stormed off. So embarrassing! Two other friends have had similar experiences with their mothers who have always been extremely kind, open hearted and open-minded! I did discover that she was suffering from a urinary tract infection which can create a condition like dementia and fortunately the outrageous outbursts were soon over after a course of antibiotics! So, what can you do to keep the carers happy if your parent suffers any form of dementia and turns into a termagant overnight? Explain that your parent has a condition that does not reflect on the carer or helper and ask for their tolerance and understanding. Also have a store of boxes of chocolate and apology notes to hand!

Patience and Understanding

There is no doubt you will need to dig deep for patience and understanding when caring for the elderly and make sure you find ways to keep yourself strong and de-stress where and when you can. Also keep a strong hold onto your sense of humour – it has helped me on many occasions to bring me from tears to laughter! In the next chapter I will look at ways we can lift the energies of our patients, ourselves and our homes and find joy and love in the situations we face.

Finally, if your parent does slip into dementia you will feel grief as you lose them, so allow plenty of personal care and comfort for yourself and know that you can only give your time and kindness – dementia needs specialised care and is, for most of us, a burden too far to carry alone. in the next chapter there are several ways that you can bridge the gap between you and also bring them comfort.

To Summarise:

- Ensure you are not harmed by any change in personality
- Acknowledge that the insults are not personal but a sign of a person losing their power and control
- Set your own boundaries of how much you can give and how much you can do. Let go expectations that they will be considerate of your time and energy
- If your parent has slipped back into childhood, then kindly and firmly treat them like a child with love and consideration
- Laugh when the opportunity to do so arises, it's perfectly alright to do so and make everyone involved feel lighter

When you are faced with the scariest and craziest situations try hard to hold onto your sense of humour and know things will change, time will move on and no matter how difficult and challenging your situation is this too shall pass!

CHAPTER EIGHT:

Bring in Light and Joy

No matter how traumatic or dire your situation with your loved one it is important to find time and opportunity to bring some light and love into both your lives. Sometimes you will have to search hard for the joy but here are some ways that I used that can lighten the energies and lift the spirits of all involved.

Music and Singing

Sharon Snir, a friend of mine, turned her time caring for her mother with Alzheimer's into an opportunity to resolve their differences and to reconnect after years of discord. She wrote a delightful book about her experiences called "Looking for Lionel" (available on Amazon). She tells of the time she and her mother spent singing together and how this bridged the communication gap created by her mother's disease. I remembered this when my mother was ill and in my care, but unfortunately my singing would certainly do nothing to raise anyone's spirits! So, I used other people's voices instead! I made up a playlist of all my mother's favourites including Bing Crosby, the Big Bands of the forties and Tina Turner and her all-time favourite, Ella Fitzgerald. The music had an immediate effect on her and she would sing along with them for hours. Even if I couldn't always sit with her, I would set up my I-pad and leave her with her music knowing she was happy.

My uncle also lived to a ripe old age (99), unfortunately he lost his sight in his later years, so I set up an iPod playlist for him of his favourite music and opera and tuned his radio into Classic FM. Like his sister music proved a tremendous comfort for him too.

Sharing Memories

I mentioned previously that I would get out the photo albums to help my mother reconnect to her family who had passed on, but it was also great to use the albums to revisit lovely family times and share old stories and funny moments. I have to say, she was far better than me at remembering times long past and she had instant recall of the names of old friends and neighbours from my childhood and her youth. I filled her room with photos of the family and friends, and I created a moving picture story on an electronic photo album.

Reading, TV and Radio

We had a TV installed in my mother's bedroom and she would happily snooze through favourite soaps and we had a lovely regular carer who would read the newspaper to her and they would laugh together at the tittle tattle of the local community.

Essential Oils and Crystals

The energy of a sick room can become quite heavy, but you can change the mood instantly by burning or spraying essential oils. I have my own blend called Clear & Cleanse which is a mix of peppermint, Spanish Sage, Juniper Berry and Cedarwood – all of which are great for clearing the atmosphere of a room. Smudging, which is the burning of herbs such as Sage, will also clear a room and Frankincense burnt on charcoal is extremely affective and I would smudge my entire home every week while my mother stayed with us simply because her energy was so low I didn't want any negativity around to cause her a problem.

Crystals will instantly lift the energy of a room. You can use:

- **Turquoise** for healing
- **Amethyst** for clarity and insomnia
- **Rose Quartz** for love and peace
- **Black Tourmaline** to clear away negative energies

Just remember to cleanse in sea salt regularly as they will get overloaded.

Finding the value

Despite the difficulties you face when you care for an elderly parent, particularly if they are in your home, there is one absolute constant and that is the love and the satisfaction you experience of giving to someone who made sacrifices for you and you has made you the focus of so much of their own lives. Sometimes you need to step back from the challenges of the daily routine and see the great gift you are giving each other. To cherish and love, tend, nurture and give to someone you love is such a wonderful experience but the joy of it can get lost in the world of the sick room. Take a little time to just sit with them and hold hands and enjoy the moment – you will feel better for it!

Laughter

Don't be afraid to laugh at some of the crazy things that are said and done! If you can, find things to laugh at and share; you will find the energy lifts immediately, even if it might seem a little disrespectful. In a recent interview, Dame Julie Walters shared memories of her grandmother who lived with her family when she was young. The old lady obviously suffered from dementia, but Julie still laughs at some of the situations her grandmother got into and she regales the fun her family had when she used a pair of coal tongs to eat a boiled egg. Her grandmother was the inspiration for the many "eccentric old lady" roles she played through her acting career. Laughter is a great release for the tension and pent up anxiety that comes with the caring role and everyone involved gets the benefit. I saw the positive effect on my mother when I either got the conversation around to humorous incidents in our family history or when we put reruns on her favourite TV comedies such as Only Fools and Horses – the number of repeats didn't seem to matter.

Other experiences that can help:

- Pets. My mother loved to stroke and pet our Labradors. If you don't have dogs of your own encourage friends to bring their pets to visit for the elderly find great comfort from petting dogs
- A bird table just outside the window where they sit will give them hours of entertainment
- Fresh flowers in the bedroom and around the house will uplift the energy and bring pleasure for everyone
- Fluffy toys and hot water bottles can be great sources of amusement and comfort
- Encourage friends and family members to visit. Even the shortest visit lightens up the day for them

Thank you for sharing my journey of caring – I hope I have helped you in what can be a most challenging time.

Remember:

- Continue your own life as normally as you possibly can and keep a balance
- Get as much help as you can to relieve you
- Don't step into self-sacrifice but do what you do with love rather than duty
- Include your parent in the decision making as much as possible
- Protect your energy from the negativity of the events and people around you
- Do the best you can and avoid guilt
- Look for the positive wherever you can
- And finally – keep your sense of humour!

My love and thoughts are with you!

APPENDIX

I have recorded several videos in my Youtube Account AnneJonesHealer. Here are the links to some you may find helpful:

Helping you to clear your karma and guilt. https://youtu.be/DIPUjzZfIDM

To release tension and anxiety, to let go of a situation that you cannot control.
https://www.youtube.com/watch?v=lu0phPPd2dI

Healing stress and being overwhelmed.
https://www.youtube.com/watch?v=uOgQeKmaZZk

To help you to heal your anger:
https://www.youtube.com/watch?v=PhCoEaypjAI

The Morning Ritual to start you day strong, protected and connected:
https://www.youtube.com/watch?v=VwZikhAbHBg

Connecting to the power of Sun energy
https://www.youtube.com/watch?v=tuVYSMd0W2g

The Anne Jones' Membership Club

£10.00 per month

Joining Anne Jones' Membership Club today gives you a wonderful opportunity to explore your healing journey more deeply, and provides you with the tools you may find useful and can help awaken 'The Power of You' and attract all you need, at the time you need it.

Membership includes:

- 10% discount on all shop products!
- Access Q&A
- The Power of You series:
    - Your Spiritual and Healing Path
    - Healing with Symbols
- Anne Jones' Membership Club Zoom meet up

To join, please visit: www.annejones.org

Energy Healing Workshop

This workshop takes you step by step through the basics of how to give energy healing and guides to a variety of meditation techniques to help you and those you wish to help.

This workshop comprises of ten lessons. Each lesson contains comprehensive lessons in video, audio and written forms to guide you step by step through all you need to enhance your energy healing and meditations.

Lesson 1 – The Human Energy Body

Lesson 2 – Energy Blocks

Lesson 3 – Energy Centres

Lesson 4 – Giving Healing

Lesson 5 – Questions and Answers about Healing

Lesson 6 – Preparing for Meditation

Lesson 7 – Meditation – White Light for Self Healing

Lesson 8 – Creating a Spiritual Connection

Lesson 9 – Meditation for Healing the Planet

Lesson 10 – Meditation Tips

To enrol, please visit: www.annejones.org

Books by Anne Jones

Heal and be Healed | Being a Carer for a Loved One

Protect Yourself | Heal Yourself | The Ripple Effect

Healing Negative Energies | Opening Your Heart

The Soul Connection | The Power of You

Published by Piatkus of Little Brown Books, available from Amazon.co.uk and bookstores.

To order, please visit: www.annejones.org

Anne Jones Books

Essential Oil Products

Clear and Cleanse

Use to clear your energies or to clear the space around you. Ideal before meditation; to ease yourself into a clear mental space. Essential Oil Ingredients: Spanish Sage, Juniper Berry, Cedarwood, Peppermint

Heart Balm

Use this delightfully fragranced body lotion to help heal heartache and to attract love into your life.

The organic lotion base contains Geranium, Ylang Ylang and Rose organic essential oils.

To order, please visit: www.annejones.org

Your Healing Path Podcast Show

Your Healing Path
with Anne Jones

Join me on a journey of spiritual healing and connectivity where I can help guide you through the obstacles and challenges which may be blocking your progress. I can help you to heal the issues that are troubling you, however big or small. If you're feeling adrift, I can help you raise your vitality and sense of wellbeing, find your path and purpose, and clear the blocks that limit you both in your personal and professional lives.

To listen, please visit: www.annejones.org